Scratching Lottery Tickets on a Street Corner

poems by

Jon Bishop

Finishing Line Press
Georgetown, Kentucky

Scratching Lottery Tickets on a Street Corner

Copyright © 2018 by Jon Bishop
ISBN 978-1-63534-701-2 First Edition
All rights reserved under International and Pan-American Copyright Conventions.
No part of this book may be reproduced in any manner whatsoever without written
permission from the publisher, except in the case of brief quotations embodied in critical
articles and reviews.

ACKNOWLEDGMENTS

Different forms of "Haircuts" and "Autumn Lake" appeared in *Boston Literary Magazine*,
and "the 21st century" appeared in *Fourth & Sycamore* as "Strange Times." A version of
"The Whittler" appeared in fewerthan500.com.

"Getting Lost" previously appeared in *The Mill Pages*.

"On Reading" was the winner of the 2014 Wilmington Memorial Library poetry contest.

"A Man Scratching Lottery Tickets on the Street Corner" and "Pub" previously appeared in
The Write City Magazine.

"On 'Nighthawks'" is of course based on Edward Hopper's famous painting.

(Say it) in "Day Trip" is a reference to Elizabeth Bishop's seminal "One Art."

I'd like to offer my deepest thanks to Finishing Line Press.

I'm indebted to Kallie Falandays and Joe Kleponis for reading this collection in its early
form and offering edits and insights. Thanks to you both.

Many, many thanks to Charles Coe, Rod Kessler, Ann Taylor, and Joe Brown.

I'd also like to thank my friends and family and mentors for believing in me and supporting
my work.

Publisher: Leah Maines
Editor: Christen Kincaid
Cover Art: Jon Bishop
Author Photo: Joe Brown Digital Photography
Cover Design: Elizabeth Maines McCleavy

Printed in the USA on acid-free paper.
Order online: www.finishinglinepress.com
also available on amazon.com

Author inquiries and mail orders:
Finishing Line Press
P. O. Box 1626
Georgetown, Kentucky 40324
U. S. A.

Table of Contents

For my mom, dad, and sister.

Daybreak

The sunshine splashes across the sleepy grass. The trees stir and yawn. Insects buzz with militant authority. Will you spring from bed? Will you stay and rest your head? The clouds are parting. The sun is up. Now you get up. You don't have much time. The dew will disappear. You will miss this chance to enjoy the cool morning. Go.

Reflections

Where has the time gone?
Beats me.
Another day older.
Another day of looking
in a mirror.

Question: Why did I think
my parents and my teachers
were lying
when they told me
every single choice
I'd make in my life
would matter?

On the surface,
things are good.
Yes: they're good.
I've a wife, two kids,
a home, a job at the
insurance company.

But what of the youthful dreams—
the aspirations:
you were good!—
of becoming a singer,
like so many others have?

I moved forward,
didn't think.

I assumed I'd be
shopping at the mall,
singing as I did so,
and some agent
would find me

and tell me how I should
immediately sign with him
so he could get a record deal.
After all,
I was perfect.

Months went by. Years.
I got caught up in life.
Don't we all?

Yes, I have a family,
a job, a home, and I
have a decent salary.

But is that enough?

Blown Away

A storm blasts its hellish winds
into creaky cemetery gates
and tall pine trees,
and it rips shingles off roofs;
makes windows shake
and makes everything shake,
as if punishing us for our sins.

But I am not afraid.

I long for ancient tales
of people blown by the wind
into places that only exist
within our dreams—places
where colors drip from the sky
and animals talk and there
are still dragons roaring.
I want respite from this life.

Take me away.

Quietus

The whole world is
creaking and crumbling
and there are cracks
in the walls.

Do you hear the
trumpet blowing?

The terrible and fierce
sound echoes
throughout the land.

Blow, blow, blow.
There is nothing
we can do.

Time is always working
in the silence
and now has turned its
piercing gaze
toward us.

Look up at the sky
and see how it has
filled with blood.
And wait. And wait.

Blow, blow trumpet.
Blow, blow, blow.

A Man Scratching Lottery Tickets on the Street Corner

A man stands in front
of the corner liquor store,
holds tickets in his hands,
scratching away, scratching,
as pedestrians walk by,
pay him no mind.

He takes off the silvery coating,
reveals the numbers underneath,
shuts his eyes for a moment,
and breathes.

Nothing.

He surrenders them to the goddamn wind.

They swerve into the clouds,
like lost birds,
and he enters the crowd again,
shuffling back to work
from lunch.

In Limbo

The streets bleak and the sky dim—
a woman stands on the curb.
Head covered and purse in hand.
The shrinking shadows
darken her face, ominous.
She's motionless.

A truck slams by and she waits for it to pass.
She contemplates moving. Lifts her foot.
Stops. Frightened, she waits more.
In limbo. In limbo.

Old

I'm old now—
I can see it
in the looks
the kids give me.

At 47, I'm an
afterthought,
some kind of
has-been—and
they speak in code
around me, but
it's code I know,
because I used
the same words
around my parents
and teachers, who
also used them
when they were young.

The things they're
talking about—going
to parties, drinking
until three, lying on
the beach and looking
at the stars—are
memories for me now,
hallucinations, even,
and all I can do is
shut my eyes and
pretend I'm there again,
as if I'm not hurtling
forward, year after year.

The 21st Century

Be great, we tell
our children.

You can do anything.
Reach for the stars,
we say. Try it all.
The world is yours.

But then,
as they grow up,
we quietly—
but with force—
step on their
aspirations,
shuttling them off
into jobs that pay
well but don't do
much for the soul.

There are smashed
writers, painters,
musicians, actors
all working at your
local office, all who
bear their lives
with dignity but who often
sit at home, in the middle
of the night, perhaps
with a few drinks—
the family is asleep; no one
will know—and can't
help but think: why?

Pieties

Refrain: The worst thing
people can tell you
is no. So what are you
waiting for?

But such pious advice
is never there for you
when you spend four
years of your life
studying for a degree
in hopes of getting
a job at a major company,
only to lose out continually
to the girl or guy who went
to the Ivy League school or
who had connected parents; and
then you have to get rid
of everything you've dreamed
of and settle for something you
hate; and then you look out
the window and see buildings
quake and then crumble to
the ground, which gives way.
The trees turn to ash,
and so does the sky.

'No' isn't the worst thing
you can hear.

Real Conversations

Yellow cabs flood the city streets
as people crowd the sidewalks
waiting for a ride.
It's one of the few places
where you can actually find
someone who wants to talk.
Not just pretend.

Not 'how's the weather?' and
'what do you do?' and 'cool.'
or 'nice' or 'yeah, I have a friend
with that name,' but real, honest

conversation. And then
the ride is over. You pay
your driver and leave.
You start walking toward
your destination
as your former driver
counts the cash. Then
he, too, departs and
everything
continues on,
seemingly unnoticed.
The cab fading among the others—
If you had a camera
and
panned out, you'd see a sea
of yellow, almost miming
blood.

People Used to Live There

In that house near the grocery store,
the one now boarded up, silent,
overgrown with weeds,

I'd always see people filtering
in and out—relatives kissing,
hugging; there would be cars
packed with family and friends.
They'd honk before they left,
before they'd say goodbye.

They loved to host barbeques,
especially on the Fourth of July.
They'd go out to the front lawn,
sit on their towels and chairs,
sip beer, and snack on hot dogs,
hamburgers, chips, and they'd laugh
as they'd watch the fireworks burst
light into a blackened sky.

But those barbeques are gone,
as are the towels and chairs.
There are no more loving goodbyes.
There are no more honks.
Only that silence.

The Beach

"Twenty minutes of exercise will be
good for you, Bill," were his doctor's exact words.
You're eighty, he said, and you need
to think of your blood pressure.

Bill didn't mind.
Every afternoon,
when the sun began
to fade, he would
head to the lake
at the center of town
and make his way
to a bench right
by the beach.

He watched the
volleyball players and
the swimmers and
always sighed.

This was stuff he
could no longer do.

Then he would shut his eyes
and he'd be twenty again.
He'd be resting on the sand,
holding a beer, taking in
the volcanic gasps
of color in the darkening
sky, surrounded by
friends long dead.

On 'Nighthawks'

Late at night, we
don't know the hour,
three of them sit,
attended to by a waiter.

Two, we think, are
a couple. She's in a
bright red dress,
has red hair, too—
it's done up
and shining, like
she's just come from
a movie premiere.
He's in a smart gray
suit and clean hat,
seems confident,
poised, and
could be someone
of distinction.

They sit close by
and chat amicably
with the waiter, who
is bending over to
refill their drinks.

But what about the man
at the far end
of the restaurant, the
man no one seems
to have noticed, the
one they
are ignoring?

The one who is alone.

He stares down, is

slumped over.

And we don't see
his face.

What there lies buried?
What has he lost?

A Poetics of Dreaming

A sharp intake of breath.
That dream again.
The one where she
leaves in a fit of rage—
leaves me standing,
open-mouthed, in the
middle of the kitchen.

Cold. AC is on.
My heart starts
beating, beating, beating.
Did it happen?
I reach over. I feel for her.
Try to touch her.
She's gone.
Oh, my God.
What now? The drinking?
The late nights?
My bed is a mess.
I kick my legs.
Tangled in the sheets.
I rip off the covers,
slam them onto the floor.
I punch the mattress.

But then I hear
feet on hardwood.
She comes running.

"Are you OK?"

Just a dream,
I want to say.
Things are fine.

Everything is fine.
But I pause.
I feign sleep.

Getting Lost

I was supposed to meet them
five minutes ago.
And now it's ten, twenty.
Soon it'll be forty, fifty.
An hour. Damn it.
And why does this always
happen to me? I'm lost.
I'm breathing heavily.
Stop. Relax. And my heart
is banging in my chest.
Slow down. You'll have
palpitations. I'm grabbing
the steering wheel,
and my hands are white.
Don't—you'll raise your
blood pressure.

Cool it. The movie is nearly over.
You've missed it. Too late.
So look around. See
the spilled canvas of a sunset.
Watch the streetlights slowly
flick on. Smile at the people
holding hands as they head
to the park. Laugh. Do it.
Laugh and laugh and laugh.

Haircuts

I've been getting haircuts
from the same barber
for twelve years now.

He knows my style and my name.
I love coming in, sitting down, and
then he flaps the protective
towel-thing; the hair flies to the floor.
I smile at myself in the mirror.

My hair is ragged and unkempt,
but not for long. I tell
him, "I'd like one
Regular haircut please."

He begins the process of
cutting, styling, snipping.
We converse during.
And about everything:
politics, the town,
the weather. Good conversation.

With the haircut complete, I look in the mirror.
Looks good—wonderful, actually.

I pay him, give him a nice tip.
He sends me off with a booming, hearty,
"Come back soon! It's been nice seeing you."
And he means it.

I leave. Go back to doing.
I return some months later.
Another haircut—a necessary
one, bringing order to my life.
Harmony.

I'm shocked—it's gone.

The barbershop is gone.
He must have retired, the barber.

In its place is one of those big,
big fancy stylist-salons.
I look at it, into it for a moment.
And I can't bear to go in.

I walk back to the car.

California

I'm a bad New Englander.
I hate the snow that
cuts your skin like
shards of glass.

I can't stand the cold,
the bitterness in the air
that seems to enter the
minds of everyone around you
and makes them bitter, too.
And miserable.

I hate the sullen trees,
the apocalyptic sky,
the hellish, deafening
quiet.

Just give me heat,
July, trips with friends,
laughter on grassy hills,
and days
that never seem to end.

Day Trip

I am on a bus amidst darkness and rain,
heading away from the city for a day.
It's a short trip, so I won't go insane
from boredom. The weathermen say
it's supposed to be like this for the hour.
I'm seeing my mother, a woman who
is of course *really* (say it) nice, but who has the power
to make me upset and angry. It's true.
I haven't spoken to her in years.
I last saw her when my father died.
Right now, I'm filled with all sorts of fears.
If we fight, at least I could say I tried.
And then back home I'd go.
Life doesn't always go as planned. I know.

Summertime Fair

It's getting late.
Time to leave,
we say.

Says the carny:

Stay. Don't go.
Just give it
five more minutes.

You can take a walk
along the shoreline
and listen to the
lapping water
as it rolls
across the sand.

You can play
a few more games.
Try your luck.
Smash those bottles and
win a prize.

Or:

Hop on the Ferris wheel
and spin, spin, spin.
Smile at the clouds.
Feel eternity.
Watch the colors
of the sunset
drip down the sky.

Midnight Revelations

It's 1950 again!
Look: you can buy
dinner for only
a few cents.

And look!
Everyone is so
neat and clean and
pressed, and there
are cars with bright
colors and tailfins.

And did you see
that sign over there?

The sock hop is at
7:30 p.m. sharp.

Don't be late!

But don't come by
around midnight,
because dad will be
on his way back from
the bar. And he won't
want to be disturbed
after a hard day's
work, no. And you'd
better shut up and leave
him alone, or else he'll
hit you again, hit you
hard—and do you want
a black eye again?

Do you want to go up
to your room again,

crying, wishing you'd
never been born?

Shopping

People float in and out of stores
holding bulging
bags of things,
clinging to them as if
the bags were
preventing them
from floating away.

Shoppers talk; they smile.
And some are alone,
meandering the seas
of stores, of booths—
would you like to
buy an electronic
cigarette? He asks.
No, thanks. They
keep moving.

As they walk,
televisions, iPads,
and radios fly out
from entrances, switch
on, and shout about
low prices and great
deals and ask if
anyone is interested
in purchasing gift cards.

No, the shoppers say.
And they keep going.

Now a few have
stopped and are sitting
on the couches
arranged like those
in a living room.

They have a reflective look
in their eyes.

Reflective, expectant—
and somewhat lost.

Have they spent
too much?

Are they regretting
the trip to the food court?

Or have they been
caught by the sirens
of the new clothes
store and as such wish
to buy stylish new shirts
and pants—the height of
fashion—even if they
cannot afford them?

Frayed by Time

In the moments
frayed by time
there is the past
and it continues
to remain,
even as we ignore it.

But sometimes
it escapes,
especially during drinks
on those warm
summer nights,
when all things seem
especially tinged with life,
and memories dance
like ghosts within
the nighttime trees.

Alive

The red buds
on the naked trees
are like scarecrows
against a monolithic sky.

Birds chirp
in the distance, as if
calling the sunrise into being.

The street lights go out.
People open their windows.

The sky brightens,
turning every shade:
A chromatics of morning.

Snowfall

The sky has turned grey.
Look upward—
past the clouds.
In heaven music
is playing, and souls are
dancing, dancing.
They twirl;
they spin and dip,
go high and low.

Someone, somewhere:
"Louder now,
and raise your glasses
into the air."
All cheer, sending
bits of the floors
and the walls
down to the earth below.

The Overlook

Often, at night,
in the summertime,
I'll drive up to the
overlook and stare
down at the city, still
engulfed with light,
with life, even though
many of its residents fell
asleep long ago.

And then I'll shut off
the radio and look out
at all those people,
take in the silence—and I'll
wonder who rose into
ebullience and who drew deeper
into darkness.

The Whittler

I whittle away at the unshaped wood in my hands as the sun sets above. The day is fading. Soon it will be dark. Hungry animals will emerge from the woods. There's no fence to protect me; I have no neighbors. My cabin sits near a lowly dirty road that carries only the occasional car. Drivers don't stop to see me. I'm an old man.

Long ago, I was paralyzed—an old war injury. I figured it'd do me some good to get out of the city and move to the country: northern Alaska. It's what you see on all the postcards. The air and trees and rivers all sparkle with untouched purity. Nothing looks poisoned.

The people who come here are those who wish to be alone. It takes a special soul to deal with the unending chill of winter. To endure, one must realize there's solace in the quiet.

The sun continues to slowly sink below the mountains. Consequently, I am bathed in a dull green glow. I hurry to finish. I'd like to make a bird in flight. It's beautiful, serene, indicative of the Alaska I see every day when I go outside to collect the mail. The sun's bright. The wind blows. The birds chirp sweet songs as I walk into my house. I sit and woodwork. I sell what I can and I move on to the next piece. I tinker with timber. My soul runs in the sap of the hardwoods and I can see this as I shape them.

Getting darker. I need to give this bird flight. I slide my knife into the sides of the block and send shavings everywhere. Soon, feathers feel ruffled and beaks, hard. I grant the bird eyes so he can know where he travels. I give him feet to walk. I carve him a tail so he may be guided. I smooth his head into clarity in order to anchor the spirit.

Now the sun casts nothing but a dim light across the woods—like a flashlight in a dark parlor. The temperature continues to cool and the wind starts to blow. I shiver. A few more cuts and slices. Now, the bird is done. I make him a mantle. I don't need to paint him. The act of flight is enough. I place him on a shelf right in front of my main window.

The sun is gone. It is time to sleep. I'm an old man. I don't need to stay awake. I wheel myself into my room and try to pull myself from my chair, but I can't. I fall with a painful thud.

My nurse—the one who cares for me—left hours ago. No matter. I need my rest, for it is time for me to sleep. I shut my eyes. Yes, time to sleep.

Those Nights

I hate those nights
where you can't sleep
and your mind races
and you think of
bills and taxes
and whether she
will leave you in
the morning and
the shadows seem
larger and the
noises outside
closer and your
breathing starts to
quicken and you
tell yourself to
just relax and
calm down, just
relax and calm down,
but you can't.
You can't.
You never can.

Trucking

One time, Rick—
a trucker, who had
spent the past forty-eight
hours driving—decided
to stop in a diner
at
the side of a long
and lonely freeway
that meandered through
the hills of the
western
part of the state.

He'd ordered French toast,
which he cut into small bites—
just like Tommy, whom he
missed terribly
and rarely got to see,
would want.

Rick remembered when
he and Monica first
introduced their son
to French toast.

"What's that gross
thing?" Tommy asked.

"You'll like it."

"Blech."

But he did.

Small bites, with
lots and lots of
syrup, too.

He ate in silence, letting
the memory overtake him,
and then he quietly paid
the bill and left.

He had more driving to do.

Unattached

My weatherman
says there
will be a meteor shower
tonight—a nice respite
from the hot and repetitive
late August days.

At midnight I step out
into the humid evening air
into the middle
of a scherzo
played by insects,
and I look

up and I see hundreds—
no, thousands—of them,
and they are gliding
and roaring across

the void and some
of them even crash
into one another and
then I remember
that I am not alone.

Light Showers

The rain falls pitter patter
on to the kaleidoscoping
infinitely soft greengrass
and I can't help but see
similarities to us in those
ricocheting little beads
of water.

And as they crash
into little explosions
I'm begging the sun
to take a breather
for just one more day.

On Spring

Spring tonight has announced its presence
in reds, in oranges, in pinks and in purples,
and it turns the sky into spilled paint,
or perhaps an explosion, and the sun is
brighter, too, as if newly-born.
It bursts like a volcano, sending fiery
yellows onto the earth and throughout space,
and we know that winter has died,
at least for the moment.

On Reading

It is late, dark, and the house
is
silent, and so I have decided
to
sit out in my living room,
in the chair that leans all the way
back; in my hands I have a book

I am halfway
through, and I've just gotten
to the good part—where the
lovers kiss, where all stories
have been drawn into
the abyss—and I go deeper,
deeper still, and if others awoke,
perhaps to get a drink of
water,
they would not see me,
for I have been transported
far, far way, into something
extraordinary.

Prayer

Crickets chirping in the evening.
The air is cool; there is a breeze.

I am walking through the park—
you know the one—
and I am watching time
tick tick tick by.

I am alone. But not really,
for I sense your presence
everywhere.

Question: Who am I?
Do I know? You do.

Talk to me.

Things dim. One by one,
streetlights flick on.

I stop, sit on a bench, cross my legs.

The jingle of an ice cream truck.
The bark of a dog.

I take a breath. And then another.

Here amidst the purple and gold sunset.
Here in the dark.

I am listening.

Stood Up

She's checked her watch
every five minutes—
it's 11:30 p.m. now,
and he was supposed
to be here an hour ago.

A sigh. She sinks.
Thinks: I should
have known.

She looks around
for sympathy—
a nod, a frown,
a kind glance.

But people rush by.
They don't notice.

She walks back
to her car,
head low,
the sound
of tires rushing
over wet pavement
her only company.

What Could Have Been

Dutifully, he arrives
everyday
at 9 a.m.
and says hello
to his coworkers,
stopping at each
of their cubicles,
asking about their
evenings.

And then he
gets to work:
sending e-mails,
making phone calls,
attending afternoon
meetings, breaking
for coffee and for lunch.

My sales are high
this month, he thinks,
and maybe I'll get a
bonus. I need it.

Because he wants to
travel to England
and walk around
London, and he wants
to see things like
the Globe Theater.

It brings back memories
of his time as a student,
when he
studied abroad in
London and had
one of his professors
tell him to try acting:

"Oh, you've got such
a good voice," she said.

So he auditioned for
a play, and he didn't
get the part, but there
was this beautiful girl
in line with him—someone
with such an extensive
resume, someone who
was definitely going places.

Long brown hair,
kind and deep brown eyes:
all adjectives apply. And he
managed to say hello and
nothing more, because he
was always afraid of talking
to women—didn't have the
confidence—and then
that was it.

She did become famous,
and he would see her face
on billboards and on television
and in the movies—and she'd
give interviews on all
the late night shows,
laughing and smiling and talking
about her start in theater
in London.

Yes, he would go to London
once per year, and he'd
imagine he actually had
the courage to talk to her
and also that he took acting

seriously, because he too
could be in the movies
or on the stage; and he
could be with her—
and they could be twirling
down the red carpet
at movie premieres,
perhaps ones they were
both in.

But he only has fantasy,
yes. There is only
what could have been,
because he only has
so much vacation time
before he has to return
to the office promptly
at 9 a.m., so he
can get his work done
and say hello to his
coworkers and ask
them about their
evenings.

Liminal Spaces

Eight p.m.
Mid-July.

You're staring
at the sky,
and you realize
you are between
darkness and light,
a liminal space
accessible
for a few
fleeting moments,
a suspension of time
you thought
only the storybooks
could achieve.

Nothing beats
the apocalyptic glow
of the sun
at late evening.

Tripping into Joy

There are times when
we are walking down the
street, and we're lost in
our cellphones and stuck
in our heads—'what's for
dinner?' or 'Oh, no. I was
supposed to meet her an
hour ago.' or 'I just made
a fool of myself at that
meeting.'—and we quicken
our pace; and we keep our
eyes away from the people
around us, away from the
flowers that are just beginning
to bloom, away from the
songbirds perched up on
the branches of those green
and tall and majestic swaying
trees. And we move quicker
still, hoping we can get home
to take a hot shower and sit
on the couch and zone out.

But then we trip.
And we fall.

We stand up and brush
our pants and our jackets
and laugh. We smile,
and take a deep breath,
because we've skinned
our
hands—no blood, but there
is a rash—and they have
started to sting.

We breathe again, deep

and through the nostrils,
filling our lungs to bursting.

We look at the sky,
and the sun has started to
set; and the colors are
bright and pink, like
tropical sands on some
distant beach. Our minds
empty, and our shoulders
relax, and we are so happy.
We are so, so happy.

The Neophyte

You always told me
I'd look in the mirror
and think of you, and
then I would say: Mom,
you were right — about
everything.

And that's what I am
doing right now, as
I hear my son
getting ready for
school, blasting music,
too — just like I did
at 16, making the
floors shake
and the walls
vibrate; and I remember

swearing at you, throwing
things at you, when you
asked me quite calmly
to turn it down.

I did the same when
you'd give me advice,
when you'd say "I have
been there before." And
that's when you'd give me
that look, the one that
admonished me for
not listening; you
knew, after all, I'd
skid into the same
things you and dad faced.

But I'm nervous, mom.
It's just me

and my son,
and you are not
here to help me out.
So I'll let the walls
vibrate and the floors
shake, as I try
to recall everything
you told me.

The Corporal Works of Mercy

I can't bury the dead—
not while she's all
around me.
There are
pictures of her on the walls,
and in my closet, though
my family and friends
told me otherwise,
I still
have her dresses, which
are slowly collecting dust,
turning the blues
and the
reds and the yellows all
into pale greys.

How can I bury the dead
when there are videos of us
laughing together, some
of which exist infinitely
and eternally on social media,
stuff that I am too afraid
and
too unwilling to delete, no
matter how hard I want to?

And how can I bury the dead
when sometimes, late at night,
when I am alone in bed and
unsleeping, I hear the wind
rustling through the leaves
and look out the window
and see the creeping dark,
the glowing moon, and then
I can hear her softly calling?

Your Heart Sinks

We've made love cheesy,
a warm-fuzzy thing.
We've
placed it
on cheap greeting cards,
made it central to the B-movies
that stroll across the networks
in the early hours of the morning.

But love can hurt. Oh,
can it hurt. Sometimes,
love is walking under
a tree and having a falling
icicle stab your heart, and
as you stand there shocked,
you try to pull it out, but
it won't budge.

Or love is being across
the country, in the middle
of finishing dinner,
and getting a
phone call from your sister,
and she tells you through tears
your father is on his last breath.

And sometimes, love is
channel surfing late at night,
and you stop because you see
a beautiful girl on the television,
and not just any girl, but one
who seems like a fairy tale,
one with silky brown hair
and bright blue eyes, a girl
who would have made even
Narcissus weak in the knees.

And as you sit there transfixed,
you hope she'll turn and notice you,
flash you a bright smile, or maybe
even reach out of the screen
and grab your hand
and pull you away.

But then your heart sinks. Your
whole body does. You know this
can never be real, because she
is only an image, one you
must turn off, no matter
how much you
can't bear to go back to
watching sunsets alone.

Autumn Lake

I'll start by saying this: I'm young, but I'm not. Thirty feels old, and I understand I have a long way to go. But I don't care. Everything seems to be on autopilot.

In college, I used to go to this lake with friends. We'd drink until the early morning and talk about our lives and then stumble back to our buildings. Once I brought a girl here. We made love and later woke up to a purple and gold sky.

Life sped up. I haven't seen anyone since school; we all do our own thing. For a while I didn't mind.

Recently things were different. I needed to get out—away from the job and my apartment and the city.

So I decided to drive back to my school, to the lake, because I wanted to get lost in my thoughts. Tonight, the past was palpable. You could touch it, feel it.

I skipped a rock across its surface. It sent ripples in all directions and bounced a few feet before sinking below the water.

I inhaled the fresh air and, immediately, all of it came flooding back.

All of it—the time we slept here and were late to our classes, the time my friends and I talked about what everything meant.

I shut my eyes for a moment.

An autumn wind blew. It carried leaves, and my memories, away from the ground and into the sky and into the past.

Expenses

Every single day,
before his shift
at the gas station,
he walks to the library—
the small one
just by the department store—
and heads to the travel section
and pulls out a book
on Australia
and sees the beautiful Uluru
and smiles at the palm trees
and the squawking birds
that rest in the branches
and then he shuts his eyes.

Pub

They told me I'd be a king
if I worked hard in school.

But I'm okay
with where I am.

I'm glad I
gave up the throne.

While all you people
listen to whirring computers
and stare
out of the windows
like fish in an aquarium,

I'm clinking glasses
and slugging beers
fresh out of the tap
with the best storytellers
on the planet.

Jack wants to tell us
about the time
he survived a plane crash,
so I order another round.

Jon Bishop was born in Winchester and raised in Wilmington, Massachusetts. His writing has appeared in a variety of publications, including the *Sentinel & Enterprise, the Arts Fuse, Boston Literary Magazine,* and *Fourth & Sycamore.* He holds undergraduate degrees in political science and English literature and a Master's in English literature. Before focusing on creative writing and poetry, he worked as a journalist for four-and-a-half years. This is his first book.

www.ingramcontent.com/pod-product-compliance
Lightning Source LLC
Chambersburg PA
CBHW021203090426
42740CB00008B/1216